KUNSTHAUS ZÜRICH

1

2

3

4

5

6

7

8

9

12
13

10

14

11

15

16

20

17

21

18

19

22

30

31

28

32

29

33

ditorial

Dear Friends of the Arts,

After a construction period of five years and four months, the extension to the Zürcher Kunsthaus is finished. What has emerged is an elegant, clearly articulated cube that is suffused with light and stands confidently on Heimplatz. Very soon, masterworks by Monet and van Gogh, by Sigmar Polke and Fischli/Weiss, by Agnes Martin and Pipilotti Rist will move in. However, for a few weeks, until the environment for the pictures and sculptures has been perfectly calibrated, it is the building itself that stands out as the real work of art.

The extension by David Chipperfield Architects is worthy of a museum for the 21st century. Not only does it bestow upon art an ideal setting and framework – ranging from the lighting to the microclimate to safety and security – but by virtue of the publicly accessible entrance hall, the art garden and the versatile usability of the studios it also reinforces art education, interactions and participation. As the title of this publication affirms: the new Kunsthaus is a museum for art AND public alike, also including an audience that may have engaged little with art up until now. This is what the voters of Zurich said yes to at the ballot box in 2012.

The extension transforms the Kunsthaus Zürich into Switzerland's largest art museum and anchors Zurich's position as a city of culture. The extension has been made possible by the initiative of the Zürcher Kunstgesellschaft, thanks to whose efforts – in addition to the contributions by the City and Canton of Zurich – a remarkable proportion of the building costs has been financed by private parties.

We would like to express our gratitude to all those involved, and we are delighted to be able to look forward to a Kunsthaus brimming with life and art. Step by step it will begin running next year, in 2021; meanwhile, this publication affords you the chance to discover the new Kunsthaus in advance. We wish you pleasant anticipation and much enjoyment in reading this volume!

[2] **Walter B. Kielholz,** President of the Einfache Gesellschaft Kunsthaus-Erweiterung and President of the Zürcher Kunstgesellschaft

[3] **Corine Mauch,** Vice President of the Einfache Gesellschaft Kunsthaus-Erweiterung and City Mayor

TABLE OF CONTENTS

'Art is vital for the life (and survival) of society. It binds and brings us together. Art acts independently of nationalities, religions or borders. With the Kunsthaus extension Zurich profits from a new, attractive art space that is accessible to all.'

—
[4] **Heike Rindfleisch,** long-standing member of the Zürcher Kunstgesellschaft, loves to be inspired and is passionate about art.

12

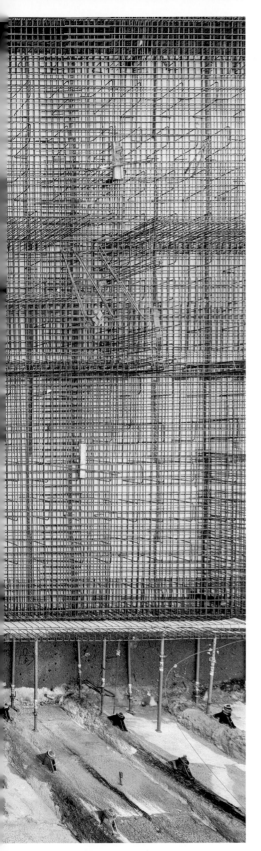

'I first saw the extension as a structural shell, but even on that tour it was already imposing. Up-to-date events demand high technical standards, and the basic equipment in the ballroom is quite impressive. But experiencing something live involves a lot of different factors. The Kunsthaus certainly scores points with its central location, its new outdoor area, and with the purist design in combination with the potential to incorporate art in symbiosis with the staging.'

—

5 **Gabriela Huber-Koller,** Head of Creation at standing ovation ag, is interested in the possibility of hiring the ballroom.

'The extension to the Kunsthaus Zürich was an essential step to allow our art museum to position itself as one of the top museums in Europe in the 21st century. Happily, eighteen years ago the city parliament shared the proposal.'

—

[6] **Robert Kaeser,** former member of the city parliament (FDP); in 2002, together with Peter Stähli-Barth (SP), he presented a motion calling for an extension to the Kunsthaus.

'I'm looking forward to the new Kunsthaus because the modern
building establishes an exciting contrast with the Old Town.
The numerous interesting museum visitors will undoubtedly
enliven our neighbourhood.'

—

8 **Peter Rothenhäusler,** President of the Quartierverein Zürich 1
rechts der Limmat, appreciates it when new perspectives are
created in the Old Town.

'This far from everyday project was subject to public submission laws.
In procurement-law terms, many of the around 450 tenders –
for example for the building's natural-stone facade or the special
large inside doors – were exciting challenges. That's why I'm
very pleased that, together with the project management, we were
able to finish the planning and the realisation without a single
contracting complaint or the associated additional delays.'

—

7 **Jürg Oetiker,** Head of the Specialist Procurement Unit of the City
of Zurich's Building Surveyor's Office, was involved, with his
team, from the beginning of the project in the processing of all
tendered contracts.

'I'm very optimistic about the cultural mile emerging on Rämistrasse. Established and young galleries on the same doorstep as the new Kunsthaus, the Schauspielhaus and the Opernhaus – where can you find a comparable concentration of cultural qualities in the very heart of a modern European city, other than here?'

—
9 **Victor Gisler's** Mai 36 gallery is located on Rämistrasse; he has dedicated himself to international contemporary art since 1988.

'What I particularly like about the new building is the combination of brass and marble, which has a very elegant effect. These materials are already there in the original Kunsthaus, which means we've got matching cleaning products. My secret formula: don't polish the brass, so that a nice patina builds up. And, marble and descaling agents never mix!'

—
10 **Paula Santos** has worked for twenty-two years as a cleaner in the Kunsthaus Zürich and knows every door handle like the back of her hand.

...ok part in the tour when the building was still a skeleton, and I was ...ty overawed. It starts with the entrance and the huge staircase ...goes on to my favourite room (the colourful small one right at the ... To me the architecture is lavish, clear, modern and impressive. ...nitely equal to the art treasures that are going to be shown there. ...n hardly wait to encounter the rooms for the first time with the ...orks in them, and am really looking forward to the opening.'

...anet Mueller, an artist from Zurich, attended a building-site tour ...utumn 2019.

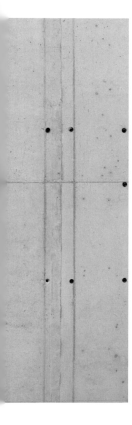

'The Schauspielhaus Zürich is similarly involved in an impassione[d] discussion about how to rethink the future of the theatre for the city. The discussions are ongoing but are nonetheless still in their infancy. Therefore: congratulations – mission accomplished! Des[pite] the spatial constraints of the city, the new Kunsthaus manages to create so much space for art, including radiating beyond the cant[on] – and with it the visibility and participation of local, national and international artists and curators. We'll keep our fingers crossed that the skateboarders from the opposite forecourt, and Naegeli, move with you, or rather that new Naegelis appear. When that happens we'll really know things are going on here – and in excitin[g] proximity to old and new galleries, to a stimulating restaurant scen[e] in Hottingen, to the Neumarkt and to the Schauspielhaus.'

—

12 **Benjamin von Blomberg** and 13 **Nicolas Stemann,** Artistic Direc[tors] of the neighbouring Schauspielhaus Zürich, are looking forward to the reinvigoration of Heimplatz.

'Due to the excellently insulated building shell and the use of geo-thermal power, solar energy and a considerable power of thought, the first art museum has been created that achieves the goals of the 2000-Watt Society.'

—

[15] **Christian Polke,** an external expert from the company Polke Ziege von Moos AG, was commissioned to oversee the building services.

'Classic beauty, rhythmic structure, integrative interpretation, hot-spot on Heimplatz, flexible carpenters' workshop with a light well in the form of an ellipse – altogether an exciting new workplace!'

—

[14] **Johann-Christoph Knospe,** a master carpenter, has been employed at the Kunsthaus Zürich since 2013.

21

'The City of Zurich has much to thank for the past political-cultural endeavours of the partnership between the FDP and SP. We were unfortunately unable to bring Sol LeWitt's 'Cube' to Zurich, but as a result, almost 20 years ago now, policy-makers were able to launch the Kunsthaus extension. Warm congratulations: the Chipperfield building is both functionally and aesthetically coherent!'

—
17 Peter Stähli-Barth, former member of the city parliament (SP); eighteen years ago, together with Robert Kaeser (FDP), he filed a motion for an extension to the Kunsthaus.

'You can already form an impression of the magnificent new building on Heimplatz from the outside. And the spacious interior, bathed in light, with its imposing stairway, can easily rival its competitors abroad. But it's only in interaction with the art that we'll see whether the new Kunsthaus is a success. I'm looking forward to the opening and am curious to see what happens.'

—
16 Patricia Siebenmann, owner of Siebenmann Communications and a long-standing member of the Zürcher Kunstgesellschaft.

'The lighting arrangement plays a crucial role in how visitors perceive the works of art. Every museum cultivates its own style of lighting; in the extension to the Kunsthaus Zürich the works are to be emphasised by being individually accentuated. Because of the rapid development and the huge advantages in quality, the originally planned lighting was entirely replaced by a new concept using LED lighting. One major focal point in this planning was the development of high-quality lights so that the colours of the exhibited works can be viewed as authentically as possible.'

—
18 Hanspeter Keller, an external specialist from the company matí AG, was commissioned to oversee the lighting design.

What took place behind the scenes?

Museum Director Christoph Becker on the expectations and realities of the Kunsthaus extension

IT'S SAID THAT FOR THE GROUNDBREAKING OF THE KUNSTHAUS EXTENSION YOU SIMPLY WENT OVER TO THE GROUNDS OF THE CANTONAL SCHOOL YOURSELF. WASN'T THERE AN OFFICIAL CEREMONY?

The staff organised an informal toast on the future building site in 2015. It was a symbolic groundbreaking back then, because after all the twists and turns and the long wait we all felt that things should finally get started. To me, the whole process, from the concept to the finished building, lasted far too long. Two decades for a public building – just try to imagine how much time, energy and money would be, and was, needed in such a wealthy city to be able to afford the luxury of taking so much time. I'm sure lessons will be learnt, and for instance faced with other major projects, that some thought should be given, after a referendum, about the right of associations to appeal.

BUT THE IDEA TO EXTEND THE MUSEUM WAS LAUNCHED BY THE KUNSTHAUS?

The first concept originated in 2001 following a public meeting at which the possibilities for expansion were discussed. And indeed the Kunsthaus extension was part of the 'specification sheet' in my employment contract with the Kunstgesellschaft in 2000. The project was and is determined by the contents. The form emerged, as it were, from the content: more space for the needs of the public; additional room for contemporary art and current art forms, for the new interaction between art and the public; additional floor space for commercial amenities, such as a bar, a shop and a ballroom; as well as the incorporation and contextualisation of a number of significant private collections. On the whole it was a highly strategic endeavour.

THE BUILDING IS INTENDED TO HAVE BEEN BUILT FOR ART AND THE WIDER PUBLIC, BUT IN 2012 ONLY 53.9% OF THE PUBLIC VOTED IN FAVOUR OF IT. A DISAPPOINTMENT?

No, it was a yes to the new Kunsthaus. Otherwise a great opportunity for Zurich would have been squandered.

WHAT DO YOU THINK SHOULD HAVE BEEN DONE TO INCREASE APPROVAL?

In terms of the financial volume of the building costs covered by the taxpayers and the corresponding maintenance and running costs, which were likewise part of the referendum, the result was to be expected. Zurich did things right by telling people straight away how much such a striking extension would cost.

WHO TURNED OUT TO BE VITAL FOR THE REALISATION OF THE WINNING PROJECT?

From the very beginning, the staff. I asked them to openly discuss the winning design, and they said: the design is great; it takes account of our operational processes. And in the end it worked. Happily, the City of Zurich and the Kunsthaus have been given a tailor-made house – by David Chipperfield.

SINCE THE PRESENTATION IN 2002 ATTITUDES TOWARDS INSTITUTIONS HAVE BECOME MORE SCEPTICAL. DID YOU EVER DOUBT THE CONCEPT?

I occasionally heard that the Kunsthaus lacked a 'vision'. But I don't deal in visions. The project adheres to a master plan with innumerable parameters that were meticulously synchronised with each other and that I, together with the team, worked through step by step. Some of the parameters involved a plan B, but on the whole numerous critical points had to be dealt with scrupulously and with the goals in mind. And that's what we successfully achieved.

CAN YOU EXPLAIN ONE OF THESE PARAMETERS AS AN EXAMPLE?

The interview with Christoph Becker was conducted on 27 July 2020 in front of members of the Zürcher Kunstgesellschaft – four months before the completion of the Kunsthaus extension and fourteen months before it becomes fully operational in October 2021. The questions were posed by Björn Quellenberg.

—

[20] **Christoph Becker,** Director, was commissioned with extending the Kunsthaus in 2000. To meet this goal he developed a plan that he then realised together with his team. On both the steering committee of the Einfache Gesellschaft Kunsthaus-Erweiterung and the Building Committee he was responsible for ensuring the Kunsthaus's artistic and operational interests.

—

[19] **Björn Quellenberg,** Head of Communications & Marketing, has been intimately acquainted with the extension project since its inception. The marketing design, communications planning and stakeholder management are all his initiatives. During the realisation he represented the Kunsthaus in the commissioning body's communications committee.

'Ultimately the Kunsthaus extension is a joint project of almost all the staff, with whom we discussed and implemented countless details.'

The fundamental principle of openness – with an over-proportional increase in floor space for the public – was clear and at the same time had to be flexible, so as to be able to absorb the imminent changes in the international museum landscape and to accomplish them through the building. We continually monitored the social and cultural-political environment and incorporated the trends into our thinking. We chose the architecture of the new Kunsthaus so that it can accommodate these transformations, both now and in the future, for more than a generation, without causing problems for the institution as a whole.

THE COMMISSIONING BODY WAS A PARTNERSHIP OF CONVENIENCE BETWEEN THE ZÜRCHER KUNSTGESELLSCHAFT AS THE OPERATOR AND USER OF THE KUNSTHAUS, THE CITY OF ZURICH, WHO AS THE SUBSIDY PROVIDER CAN IMPOSE STIPULATIONS AND FORMULATE AGREED OBJECTIVES, AND THE STIFTUNG ZÜRCHER KUNSTHAUS, WHO OWN AND MAINTAIN THE PROPERTIES. WHAT CONFLICTS OF INTEREST WERE THERE AND HOW WERE THEY SOLVED?

It was a division of labour that worked excellently, due to the participants who worked on the project over the long term, ensuring that there was no knowledge drain. The loyalty towards the project and the efficiency of the cooperation were, and still are amazing, and gave me the certainty that the project could be tackled.

COULD YOU GIVE AN EXAMPLE OF A COMPLEX PROBLEM WHERE SOLVING IT REQUIRED CONSENSUS?

To be honest there were more clear decisions than compromises. We knew what we wanted, and we clearly formulated this. This started with the question of location. To be able to sustainably operate in the long term, Heimplatz was the only choice, together with a physical connection between the extension and the existing buildings. Apparently this was a convincing approach in that there were no fundamental disagreements. The architects also played a role in that they proved to be readily cooperative and innovative about a series of delicate issues, including details such as a

25

digital information wall screen in the entrance area. It wasn't a best-of request show; instead everything went according to plan.

WHO GAVE YOU UNEXPECTED SUPPORT?

The many private donors who have supported our project, some of them very, very generously, and almost all of them come from Zurich. This surprised and emotionally touched us over and over again. As a side effect you come to recognise those people who pretend to be generous but keep their bulging wallets closed. But that was always a rare exception.

WERE THERE ANY TABOO SUBJECTS WITHIN THE PROJECT ORGANISATION TEAM?

No. Taboos are obstacles that shouldn't be tolerated. We countered opposition with arguments. Even if you can't please everybody, the approval is greater today than ever. And I'm happy, despite certain attempts to stymie us, and occasional attempts to stir things up, that we stayed level-headed.

DISASTERS, MISHAPS AND SETBACKS ARE PART OF ANY BUILDING SITE. WHAT ABOUT IN YOUR CASE?

As a matter of fact the construction process went entirely smoothly, due to the steady-handed organisational talents of the Building Surveyor's Office, the architects, and the users, in other words ourselves. Above all the project managers from the Building Surveyor's Office, the Kunstgesellschaft and, last but not least, the building managers all did an amazing job – a big compliment to them all!

DOES THE PERSONAL CHEMISTRY BETWEEN THE ARCHITECTS AND THE COMMISSIONING CLIENTS PLAY A ROLE IN IMPLEMENTING SOMETHING LIKE THIS?

The architects managed to implement what was an extremely detailed spatial programme without cutting any corners. This mirrors the specific qualities of the Kunsthaus as a museum and as an exhibition institu-

tion with international appeal. My own collaboration with David Chipperfield and with the team of architects in Berlin was always close and trusting: all my questions were processed and answered promptly. Despite the long planning and building phases, there were never any disagreements. David Chipperfield is undeniably one of the best museum architects of our era.

HAVE ARTISTS BEEN SPECIFICALLY COMMISSIONED FOR WORKS FOR THE EXTENDED KUNSTHAUS?

The concept is one of flux. Nevertheless, there are one or two works of art that we've developed with artists for particular places, for instance with Lawrence Weiner for the staircases, which lead to the passageway connecting the buildings, or with Pipilotti Rist for Heimplatz. These could be called commissioned works, but that actually only applies to how they have been financed.

WHAT ARE THE HIGHLIGHTS OF THE EXTENSION?

Definitely the impression of the entrance hall, which creates an amazingly imposing interior space and that the visitors and the Kunsthaus can use or hire for events. This space is the most visible sign of the institution's transformation and simultaneously a cultural-political statement: Come and see! This is how beautiful a house of art can be. At the same time we've also set an aesthetic standard for public civic space. Moreover, the integration of the highly important private collections and the crossover with the Kunsthaus's imposing collection is certainly a distinguishing feature, demonstrating the amazing potential of a Swiss museum.

IT SOUNDS COSY. WHERE'S THE PROVOCATION? AND WHAT ABOUT THE POTENTIAL FOR INDIGNATION?

That's not what it was about. It's about creating something for coming generations that guarantees the Kunsthaus a place amongst the international competition – quite high up the ranking, that's where it belongs, and now it can prove it.

**WHICH NEWLY PRESENTED WORKS HAVE THE PO-
TENTIAL TO LEAVE A LASTING PUBLIC IMPRESSION?**

There are a lot of works that we've been unable to
show for decades due to a lack of space, while others
have been acquired with the new spatial circum-
stances in mind. There will also be new art shown on
Heimplatz. Very little at all in the Kunsthaus will stay
where it's traditionally been; hundreds of artworks
will appear in other rooms and in a new light. There
will be surprises on both sides of Heimplatz when the
curtain rises for the collection, that's for sure.

**THE GENERAL EXPECTATION IS DADA, FILMS,
INSTALLATIONS, MORE WORKS BY FEMALE ARTISTS
AND ARTISTS OUTSIDE EUROPE …**

There's something of everything.

**LESS THAN HALF THE EXPENDITURE FOR THE
KUNSTHAUS COMES FROM THE PUBLIC PURSE,
WHICH MAKES PRIVATE REVENUES PARTICULARLY
IMPORTANT. WHAT ARE THE TARGETS IN THE
BUSINESS PLAN, WHICH WAS ALREADY DRAWN UP
IN 2011?**

The high proportion of self-funding remains as it is.
For the subsidy providers the Kunsthaus represents a
comparatively affordable institution. At the same time
the Kunstgesellschaft enjoys a certain independence,
which we certainly value.

**DESPITE THE BUILDING SITE, THE KUNSTHAUS HAS
ALWAYS REMAINED OPEN. THE STAGING OF
EXHIBITIONS HAS CARRIED ON WITHOUT INTER-
RUPTION. DOESN'T THAT DRAIN PERSONAL RE-
SOURCES, WHEN NUMEROUS DEPARTMENTS
HAVE TO WORK ON THE PLANNING AND START OF
OPERATIONS OF A MAJOR PROJECT PARALLEL
TO THEIR DAILY BUSINESS?**

That is a challenge, but also an opportunity for everyone
to get involved. Ultimately the Kunsthaus extension
is a joint project of almost all the staff, with whom we
discussed and implemented countless details. We incorporated their sometimes long-standing experience,
their ideas and their wishes for a better museum.
You can see that, and moreover people will soon notice
how well the new Kunsthaus functions and interacts
with the existing building. The Chipperfield building is
much more than a simple extension.

WHAT'S MISSING?

It's strange that such a high-ranking urban ensemble
can emerge, an urban square with interesting architecture and lots of fluctuation, but that solving the
layout of this square apparently remains an unsolvable
problem. With the opening of the Chipperfield building,
this is what a lot of people in the city think and it will
probably surprise many international visitors. Whether
a solution can be found in the foreseeable future is
doubtful, but we'll see.

**IN 2022, THE FIRST YEAR WHEN IT CAN BE JUDGED
WHETHER THE NEW KUNSTHAUS HAS REACHED
ITS GOALS, YOU YOURSELF WILL SLOWLY HAND ON
YOUR SCEPTRE. WHAT SCOPE – BOTH IN TERMS
OF PROGRAMME AND OPERATIONS – WILL YOUR
SUCCESSOR HAVE LEFT?**

An enormous amount. The building has to prove itself.
The prerequisites are now in place. The extension
makes the Kunsthaus Zürich an international heavy-
weight, in its visual appearance too. That's a challenge.
It's an establishment that deserves a competent,
strong-minded personality, someone who enjoys the
trust of policy-makers, the public and the staff.
These qualities are crucial to successfully managing
the Kunsthaus.

—
Christoph Büchel, Hausmeister
(Deutsche Grammatik) / Janitor
(German Grammar), 2008
Installation: building material and
household items
294 x 954 x 722 cm

—
Katharina Fritsch, Frau mit Hund /
Woman with Dog, 2004
polyester, iron, aluminium, paint
height: 176 cm (woman)

—
Lungiswa Gqunta, Lawn, 2017/2019
glass, floor panel, petrol, ink
336 x 483 cm

28

Christoph Büchel (b. 1966 in Basel) has made a name for himself since the 1990s with complex spatial installations and conceptual projects. The impetuses for his work are present-day socio-political questions. Büchel, a Swiss national, transposes real-world situations into the art environment, thus morphing them into model-like arrangements of the phenomena of our times. His installations are akin to three-dimensional collages, which mostly extend over a number of rooms and often have something disconcerting or worrying about them.

'Hausmeister (Deutsche Grammatik)' (2008) is the three-room flat belonging to a (fictitious) janitor husband and wife, split in half by a wall. On the one hand the work makes a controversial topic in German history vividly tangible, namely life with the Berlin Wall. On the other hand the work is based on an article that Christoph Büchel read in the tabloid 'Bild', describing a couple who had quarrelled so badly they had put up a wall in the marital flat. True to form, the personal is always political in Büchel's works.

Recently the issues of borders and walls have become particularly pressing again. Thus it is an interesting moment to show the 2010 acquisition for the first time in the extension building.

Katharina Fritsch (b. 1956 in Essen) is one of today's leading visual artists. Her works are to be found in numerous public and private collections. In the run-up to her major solo exhibition of 2009 at the Kunsthaus Zürich, the Vereinigung Zürcher Kunstfreunde acquired an important group of works by the artist thematically dedicated to the city of Paris. The purchase was made with the extension building already in mind. Finally the moment has arrived: 'Frau mit Hund' (2004) can be shown for the first time in the context of other contemporary works of art in the new Chipperfield building.

The focal point of the group of works is a woman formed out of pink scallop shells with a similarly arranged dog. These figures are coupled with sixteen coloured parasols floating on the ceiling and six large-format screen prints reproducing postcard scenes of Paris. All of the works can be exhibited individually or as a large overall installation. The group of works conveys an airy lightness and evokes associations with Rococo, French chateaux, Surrealist art, but also cheap seaside souvenirs. With 'Frau mit Hund' Fritsch manages to merge entirely contradictory worlds in a refreshing amalgam of high and low.

Lungiswa Gqunta (b. 1990 in Port Elizabeth) is a young South African artist who has attracted attention with her politically laden and formally precise spatial installations. Her works are often inspired by the socio-political context of her home country but tackle topics with global significance and ramifications – as in her installation 'Lawn' (2017/2019).

In contrast to the carefully manicured stretches of lawn that still belong mostly to the largely white upper classes in South Africa, the lawn in Lungiswa Gqunta's room-sized installation is composed of broken bottles filled with an explosive mixture of petrol and green ink, thereby creating a striking image of marginalisation and social inequality, as well as a potential act of resistance.

In the context of the restaging of the collection, the installation will be shown in the former 'Seerosensaal' (Water Lilies Gallery) in the historical Moser building. The presentation is part of the so-called 'intervention spaces', which are spread throughout all of the buildings and which critically reflect and update the collection.

—
[21] **Mirjam Varadinis,** Curator at the Kunsthaus Zürich, is responsible, together with the Collection Curator Philippe Büttner, for the new organisation of contemporary art into the collection.

Twenty Designs
for an Art Museum –
One for Zurich

— 22 **Wiebke Rösler Häfliger**, Chair of the Building Committee, Director of the City of Zurich's Building Surveyor's Office

ARCHITECTURAL COMPETITIONS AS A GUARANTEE OF QUALITY

How does good museum architecture manifest itself? Why was the concept for the Kunsthaus extension building by David Chipperfield Architects the one that was ultimately realised? Who took the decisions? These are all perfectly legitimate questions from anyone not intimately acquainted with the project. In short, the answer is: the design was selected in an anonymous architectural competition. In this way the commissioning clients ensured that the best possible project was built, rather than the next-best.

On the basis of its experience in this field, the City of Zurich's Building Surveyor's Office was commissioned to organise the competition. They elaborated the competition programme and the specific remit based on the groundwork undertaken by the project participants and the administrative offices involved. The presence of numerous historical buildings on Heimplatz and its significance as the gateway to the university district meant that high urban-planning and architectural standards applied. Of equal importance were the functional and operational aspects, due to the fact that the extension should form a unity with the existing Kunsthaus. Added to this were the goals that the project be ecologically sustainable and have a model character economically.

Of the many factors, the composition of the jury played a key role in guaranteeing a fair process. Twenty personalities from business, culture, architecture, landscape architecture, politics and administration formed the prize jury, including representatives from the project participants and independent professional experts from Switzerland and beyond. As was to be expected, the competition excited considerable international interest. From the 214 entries, the jury selected twenty teams for the next stages: nine from Switzerland, eight from surrounding European countries and three from outside Europe. Those chosen submitted their projects anonymously, affixed with a keyword. Only after three days of deliberations – when the envelopes were opened – did it become clear that the winning project, 'Aglaia', came from David Chipperfield Architects.

Since the completion of the competition I have been part of the project in my function as chair of the Building Committee, and as such responsible, together with the team of architects and a wide range of construction and operational professionals, for the development of the project. Our continuing efforts have had one goal: to nurture the design to make it fully fledged for the building stage, and then to implement it.

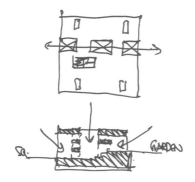

hitectural quality in
ding processes

facade model on the building
was erected to assist
Building Committee and
team of architects in finding
able materials.

atural stone was selected:
sberger limestone from
ton Basle-Country met
he specifications for
facade of the new building.

facade was carefully clad in
stone blocks, which had
n cut to size in the quarry.

PROJECT MANAGEMENT ALSO REQUIRES TEAMWORK

—
A working day in the life of the chief project manager [29] **Rahel Fiechter**

—
Due to their excellent cooperation, the project team made a vital contribution to the successful realisation of the new building – Rahel Fiechter, Chief Project Manager for the commissioning body, with Niels Hochuli, Chief Construction Manager (left), and Dag Vierfuss, User/Operator Project Manager (right).

On my way, between a coffee and the first emails, I think about the key points of my speech for the construction site tour this evening. As an architect with the city's Building Surveyor's Office I represent the interests of the commissioning clients in the Kunsthaus extension and am responsible for project management. That means, in essence: project control, the aim being to keep to the costs, quality and schedules.

—
07:30

In the office I have my first meeting with our head of procurement to clarify legal aspects of the tenders. There are about 450 tenders with 150 contracts to process.

—
08:00

I actually wanted to start on the status report for the steering committee, who need to be kept regularly up to date about the cost and scheduling developments, and about project risks and their prevention. I get interrupted by a phone call.

—
08:17

The planning team is upset because companies are seemingly not meeting their contractual performance targets, meaning a potential risk of additional costs. My further training in mediating proves useful once again.

I arrange an escalation meeting for the next day and write a formal warning and a defects notification.

—
09:30

Thanks to the rigorously run cost-management system, including control instruments, I can keep an overview. The claims for additional payments from firms and planners have to be checked; negotiation sessions are required to indemnify the clients.

—
10:00

We start the 198th project team meeting, which I'm responsible for preparing and chairing. The teamwork with the Kunsthaus Zürich's project manager, Dag Vierfuss, and the chief construction manager of the planning team, Niels Hochuli, functions very well. Due to our positional and professional skills, as well as our experience in carrying out major projects, we work hand in hand and are an efficient team. The meeting ends on time at 12 noon.

—
13:00

I finally get round to drawing up the status report. The good news for the clients: the budgeted costs of 206 million francs will be kept to, probably – there's still six months to go before completion at the end of 2020.

—
14:15

The 68th meeting of the Building Committee is pending. I discuss things with our director, Wiebke Rösler Häfliger, who chairs it. The necessary key decision-making points have been sent to the members in good time.

—
15:10

While I'm answering emails, a colleague from our Specialist Sustainable Building Unit rings up. As part of the quality management on behalf of the clients he's undertaken a building inspection that I requested, and checked whether the construction materials meet the ecological specifications. Everything's fine.

—
16:20

The notification of bankruptcy for the ventilation company comes in; the firm has stopped all work with immediate effect. I've got to act immediately and find a follow-up agreement to as far as possible avoid any scheduling delays.

—
18:00–19:00

The construction site tour is a pleasant way to end the day. Knowledge sharing is also part and parcel of a major project.

2000 WHAT?

A MUSEUM FOR THE
2000-WATT SOCIETY

—
28 **Thomas Kessler,** City of Zurich's
Building Surveyor's Office, Specialist
Sustainable Building Unit

Future visitors to the new Kunsthaus building will barely notice that the museum is a model of ecological excellence. After all, everything revolves around art and the public. In this sense the constructional and servicing interventions designed to improve its sustainability are either not immediately visible or are perceived as normal – for instance the windows, where the incoming daylight plays a key role in saving energy. In fact the underlying energy concept of the extension building goes far beyond this single example and is, in essence, decisive for the ecologically pioneering character of the new building. The basis for this are the goals of the 2000-Watt Society, which, according to the will of the voters, are politically binding on the City of Zurich. Correspondingly, these aims likewise underpinned the planning and realisation of the Kunsthaus extension.

This in turn means that the overall energy requirements for the erection and running of the building have been significantly reduced in comparison to existing museum buildings. In terms of greenhouse gas emissions this has resulted in a reduction by a factor of four, thus saving around 1,300 tonnes of CO_2 per year, which is roughly equal to 400,000 litres of heating oil. Moreover, the Kunsthaus depends entirely on renewable energy.

Comparable recent museum buildings
120 kilograms CO_2 per square metre of energy reference area per year

GREENHOUSE GAS EMISSIONS FROM THE CONSTRUCTION AND OPERATIONAL RUNNING OF THE KUNSTHAUS EXTENSION

1/4

OPERATION

CONSTRUCTION

The new Kunsthaus building
Emissions reduced by a factor of four

Building form
The compact form, in other words the advantageous ratio between the shell and the volume of the building, saves building material, thus reducing grey energy. In addition, 98% of the concrete used consists of recycled concrete with CO_2-reduced cement.

Light
Because in most museums light constitutes one of the largest 'energy guzzlers', the new museum is designed to enable a maximum amount of daylighting. On the lower floors daylight is admitted into the interior by means of generously dimensioned facade windows. On the top floor the exhibition rooms are supplied with natural lighting via large-format skylights – obviously filtered appropriately to protect the works of art. Whenever the daylight is insufficient, artificial lighting is automatically activated, suitably illuminating the exhibition spaces. Energy-saving LED technology is utilised throughout the whole building, simultaneously improving the quality of the colour rendering.

Indoor environment
Due to the solid-construction approach and the excellent thermal insulation, the building as such provides a well-balanced indoor climate. Heating and cooling are therefore kept to a minimum. Finely tuned sensors in each room of the extension building register the presence of people in them, and thanks to precise controls and sophisticated technology the delicate artworks are always exposed to the correct conditions. In order to regulate the temperature a cleverly devised system of pipes was installed in the walls and ceilings, which can supply or extract heat as needed. This occurs via highly efficient heat pumps, which use the ground beneath the building as heat or cold storage by means of a geothermal probe. This flow of heat back and forth requires only a fraction of the energy needed for a conventional heating and cooling system.

Air-conditioning
Along with supplying fresh air, the air-conditioning system is mainly responsible for the moisture balance in the museum. A precisely controlled system guarantees that each room receives the right amount of fresh air with an exactly accurate moisture content. On the one hand this ensures a comfortable environment for the visitors, and on the other it fulfils the conservational requirements for the valuable works of art. The air-conditioning installations are only operational when really needed, explaining why they necessitate only minimal energy use.

Energy
The new building runs solely on renewable energy. The electricity is generated from Swiss hydroelectric power stations. No fossil fuels, or for that matter atomic power, are used, whatsoever. Circa 10% of the energy consumption can be generated from photovoltaic installations on the roof. The remaining roof surface is used to channel as much daylight as possible into the exhibition rooms on the second upper storey, which in turn has an additional positive energy consumption effect.

35

'Pipilotti Rist, for over three decades in the video art world as the painter of coloured light and sound, a seductive activist of sensitivities and feelings, liquefied walls and corners, with gentle boldness. The moment the light and the projectors are switched on she consummates the act of digital liberation and transforms walls into flooded imageries.'

[24] Jacqueline Burckhardt

TACTILE LIGHTS

CARESSING BUILDINGS WITH LIGHT

—
[23] Nike Dreyer

As Pipilotti Rist began the preparations in 2015 for her exhibition in the Kunsthaus Zürich, her aim was to resurrect the idea of Kunsthaus architect Karl Moser, namely to accord equal space to art outside the museum. To this end she transformed a relief by Carl Burckhardt and the glazed roof of the Kunsthaus into a projection screen. Thus, in 2016, the first stage of 'Tastende Lichter' / 'Tactile Lights' emerged, and since then the installation illuminates the architecture night after night. In 2020 she expanded the work, as originally planned and again with the support of light designer Kaori Kuwabara, with a second stage. In so doing, 'Tactile Lights' connects the facades of all the adjoining buildings on Heimplatz – the Kunsthaus, the extension, as well as the Schauspielhaus theatre – and caresses them slowly with circular surfaces of light of differing configurations of colour and a new relief projection.*

Rist adjusts the relationship between light art and urban space: part of her intervention is the design of a mast that acts as a central anchoring point, both in artistic and practical terms. On the one hand the mast meets all the technical specifications of the city authorities – it encompasses all the lights designated in the city lighting concept, the 'Plan Lumière' – while on the other hand it also serves as a sculptural element. With its soft sweep, its organically shaped headpiece and its exciting play of lights, it becomes a totem of hope, especially during the daytime. Taken as a whole, what emerges is a soothing programme in which the entire Heimplatz is connected to form a single entity – at night through surfaces of light and during the day through the sculpture.

—
Drawings by [25] **Pipilotti Rist,** renderings by Mara Meerwein as well as the colour pattern c the mast with [26] **Kaori Kuwab** collage by Thomas Rhyner.

—
* The first part of the work 'Tactile Lights' in the Moser Building was realised as a commission by the Kunsthaus Zürich. The second part on Heimplatz was commissioned by the developers of the Kunsthaus extension, under the project management of [27] **Karin Frei Bernasconi,** financed from the building cre

The New Kunsthaus and the City of Zurich

The Kunsthaus extension will undoubtedly become a Zurich landmark. The Head of the Department of Planning and Building, André Odermatt, and Christina Schumacher, a professor in social sciences, explore in conversation with Anna Schindler, Director of Urban Development, how the extension building creates a new public civic space, how it belongs to Zurich and how it will have a lighthouse effect beyond the city.

Anna Schindler

THE KUNSTHAUS EXTENSION IS MORE THAN SIMPLY A BUILDING. THE INTENTION IS TO CREATE AN ATTRACTIVE PUBLIC SPACE – IN CONJUNCTION WITH HEIMPLATZ AND THE ART GARDEN. HOWEVER, BECAUSE OF THE DEVELOPMENT OF THE UNIVERSITY DISTRICT, THE NEIGHBOURHOOD WILL BE DOMINATED BY CONSTRUCTION SITES FOR THE NEXT FEW YEARS. CONSIDERING THE SITUATION, HOW WILL IT NEVERTHELESS BE POSSIBLE TO RAPIDLY DEVELOP THE ATTRACTIVENESS OF THE LOCATION FOR VISITORS AND THE PUBLIC IN GENERAL?

André Odermatt

Obviously, construction lorries are also going to stay a feature of the neighbourhood for quite a time to come. But the energy that the Kunsthaus extension has already generated is a force in itself. The new building means that the Pfauen, as a whole, is finally correctly defined: the existing Kunsthaus has a vis-à-vis, and Heimplatz becomes a real civic square.

Christina Schumacher

The new Kunsthaus and Heimplatz are a 'stepping stone' – a first step towards Rämistrasse as an educational and cultural mile. This is where the people of Zurich can see that something is about to emerge. The extension will be open to everyone next year. Heimplatz will still not have achieved its ideal form, but its transformation is more imminent. It's great for the university district that the Kunsthaus has a head start.

Anna Schindler

WHAT WE'RE SEEING ON HEIMPLATZ IS THE EMERGENCE OF A CULTURAL HUB, WHICH WITH THE EXTENSION BUILDING ALREADY HAS A HEART EVEN BEFORE THE EDUCATIONAL AND CULTURAL MILE HAS BEEN ENTIRELY REALISED. AT THE MOMENT THE NEW KUNSTHAUS STANDS ALONE. IT IS MEANT TO EMBODY A GATEWAY, WHICH AS SUCH IS STILL NOT YET TANGIBLE – NOT EXACTLY WHAT YOU'D DESCRIBE AS AN EASY URBAN STATUS.

[30] **André Odermatt** is a City Councillor and Head of the City of Zurich's Department of Planning and Building.

—

[31] **Christina Schumacher** is a professor in social sciences and the Head of Research at the Institute of Architecture at the University of Applied Sciences and Arts Northwestern Switzerland.

—

[32] **Anna Schindler** is the Director of Urban Development of the City of Zurich

'The new Kunsthaus is very much Zurich – it fits here. Discreet but nevertheless powerful.'

André Odermatt

The extension building is the prelude and the open door to the educational and cultural mile. At the moment the area around Rämistrasse is in a deep state of slumber – there are a number of cultural institutions, for instance, that enjoy little visibility. This is where the new Kunsthaus serves as an impulse. There is, of course, an element of regret: the reorganisation of Heimplatz has been delayed. Nevertheless, even if we have to wait for the perfect solution, the spatial assembly already works. Above all the openness of the extension building, its transparency, already has a radiating effect for the whole square.

Christina Schumacher

What has been done is to establish a visual connection between the buildings. However, it's still crucial that Heimplatz is freed from being a traffic intersection to become a bustling urban space. Right now people ask themselves: Heimplatz? Where's that? The square is suffocated. Whatever the reconfiguration, it has to be perceivable, even if the traffic remains. The hope has to be that the public discovers the still-hidden qualities of the square and demands more amenity value for the future, at the expense of the room given to motorised vehicles.

André Odermatt

It was a happy coincidence, emerging from the lengthy discussions about the size of the new building, that it was moved back and made smaller. This created a frontal area that gives the square air to breathe – above all with the new Kunsthaus bar's alfresco tables and chairs. With the remodelling of Heimplatz, the Schauspielhaus also gains a little more entrance space. In this respect the roads will be slightly less dominant; the nature of a square will be noticeable.

Anna Schindler

THIS ASPECT, THE SEMI-FORECOURT BAR, IS VERY IMPORTANT. THINGS ARE HAPPENING – THINGS THAT IN ANOTHER RECENT CULTURAL CENTRE, THE LÖWENBRÄU-AREAL IN ZURICH-WEST, INITIALLY

WEREN'T DONE: WHAT'S BEEN ACHIEVED IS THE CREATION OF AN EXTERNAL OPENNESS AND THE EXTENSION OF AN INVITATION TO COME INTO THE BUILDING THAT IS GIVEN TO EVERYONE.

Christina Schumacher

This is a crucial point. The new Kunsthaus is seen, rightly, as a public building, and it expresses this too. Via the public hall you can access the university district through the art garden. The building affords an entrance for a wide public. Permeability and free walkability are cornerstones for the development of the university district.

André Odermatt

The building and its public character are stylistically indicative for the university district. They give an impression of what porosity can look like.

Christina Schumacher

Our cities and towns, which are becoming ever more compact and fuller, need open inner spaces. The exchange between inner and outer spaces produces new urban territories. The Kunsthaus extension is in an ideal position to realise this.

Anna Schindler

THE EXTENSION BUILDING CREATES A NEW CULTURAL CENTRE AT THE FOOT OF THE ZÜRICHBERG. A SIMILAR ART AND CULTURAL CENTRE ALREADY EXISTS IN ZURICH-WEST, IN THE FORM OF THE ALREADY MENTIONED LÖWENBRÄU-AREAL AND THE SCHIFFBAU. OBVIOUSLY THERE'S A QUESTION ABOUT HOW THE TWO POLES RELATE AND WHETHER THE CITY IS LARGE ENOUGH FOR BOTH OF THEM.

Christina Schumacher

The two of them are very different locations. When I'm out in Zurich-West I'm on the party mile – it's fancy, the hip place to be. On Heimplatz I'm in the traditional centre of Zurich, close to the Old Town. In terms of the urban spatial layout it's crucial that these locations retain their different ambiences. Dual-poled, or even multi-poled, developments are beneficial for Zurich.

André Odermatt

There's room in the city for two cultural locations. In Zurich-West I anticipate new art, art that's at the cutting edge. I tend to go to the Kunsthaus or the Schauspielhaus to experience more, if you will, 'prestigious' events, or the fantastic art collection. It's not about 'either-or', rather 'side-by-side' – ultimately a city distinguishes itself by its diversity and not by its uniformity. Because of the different positions there's a stimulating competition. Both locations have to discover their own individual identities, develop new ideas, stay attractive.

Anna Schindler

NONETHELESS, THERE'S STILL A DANGER THAT ZURICH-WEST MAY SUFFER BECAUSE OF THE POWERFUL NEW COUNTERPART – ESPECIALLY BECAUSE THE WEST PART OF THE CITY WILL FUNDAMENTALLY CHANGE AGAIN ARCHITECTURALLY IN THE COMING YEARS.

Christina Schumacher

Personally I see it more as an impulse that all the parties actively evolve further.

André Odermatt

Some things have already changed in this respect: for example there's already a small alfresco bar-cum-restaurant on the Löwenbräu-Areal. Perhaps the competition is healthy so that the parties become aware that they have to offer more than just exciting exhibitions. But I don't think the location will suffer. Zurich-West attracts a different public; it's a location that – like every gallery, like every off-space – has to continually reinvent itself. This perhaps applies somewhat less to the Kunsthaus with its collections.

Christina Schumacher

The Kunsthaus also positions itself largely through exhibitions – it calls itself an 'art house' and not an 'art museum'. The two locations don't necessarily attract different clientele. That generates a vitality.

Anna Schindler

THE EXTENSION BUILDING IS A VERY GOOD BUIL-
DING, BUT IN A CERTAIN SENSE ALSO VERY
UNSPECTACULAR. IT'S NOT A SIGNATURE BUILDING,
LIKE FOR EXAMPLE THE GUGGENHEIM IN BILBAO
OR THE TATE MODERN EXTENSION IN LONDON,
INSTEAD IT'S VERY UNDERSTATED – TYPICAL FOR
ZURICH PERHAPS. HOW CAN THE BUILDING NEVER-
THELESS EXERT A PULL THAT EXTENDS BEYOND
THE CITY AND GIVES THE KUNSTHAUS INTERNATIO-
NAL RENOWN AS A MUSEUM?

André Odermatt

There are two elements: the one is the collections
and exhibitions that mark the Kunsthaus's status; the
other is the architecture. Bilbao has this look as if a
UFO had landed. The new Kunsthaus, by comparison,
is very much Zurich – it fits here. It works with the
shades of colour of Zurich as a city, with its discreet
sandstone. And yet despite this it's a very powerful site, one that can also be very effectively staged
through the camera lens. In Bilbao people talk above
all about the building and less about the art. That's
perhaps the difference and the great strength of
the extension building: the Chipperfield building
proffers itself to art, it itself doesn't try and grab
the limelight.

Christina Schumacher

The new building is city-specific not building-specific;
it doesn't create a spectacle and doesn't primarily
point to its own authorship. Personally I consider this
to have a more enduring effect than an exercise in signature architecture. For that reason I myself wouldn't
refer to the 'Chipperfield building'. A 'Chipperfield'
would be far less specifically Zurich-like than, for
instance, the Opernhaus annexe, humorously dubbed
the 'meat loaf'. I'm curious to see what the population
think about the extension building and what they'll
call it.

Anna Schindler

IN THE BEGINNING VARIOUS CRITICAL VOICES
COMPLAINED THAT THE NEW KUNSTHAUS RESEM-
BLED A BUNKER. NOW AN ELEGANT, DELICATE
BUILDING IS EMERGING FROM BEHIND THE SCAF-
FOLDING LIKE A BUTTERFLY FROM ITS COCOON. THE
COMMENTS FROM PASSERS-BY SHOW THAT THE
BUILDING EXCITES SURPRISE AND APPRECIATION.
NEVERTHELESS, HOW DOES ONE MANAGE TO AN-
CHOR A LONG-LASTING ACCEPTANCE FOR THE BUIL-
DING AND THE WHOLE SITE AMONGST PEOPLE IN
THE NEIGHBOURHOOD AND THE CITY AS A WHOLE?

Christina Schumacher

I think we can only answer that question when the
building opens and the public character of the
main hall becomes apparent to the visitors – when
you can see the beautiful and exquisite materials that
have been used with your own eyes and how meticulously they've been handled. The general public
need time to properly discover a building like this,
to assimilate it.

André Odermatt

Prior to starting, numerous events were held in the
neighbourhood – discussion groups, an experts' dialogue with architects. It's typical for Zurich that, to
start with, an architectural project attracts a lot of
criticism. In cases like this it's important to look for
a dialogue, especially with such major building
projects when fears quickly arise that they may
overwhelm what already exists. Precisely as a result
of this dialogue it was decided to reduce the size
of the extension building somewhat and to set it back.
These moves significantly increased acceptance in the
neighbourhood; I got a lot of positive feedback. And
to give the architects their due, they engaged with this
dialogue and responded to the feedback.

Anna Schindler

PERHAPS, IN THE END, THE NEW KUNSTHAUS
WILL UNDERGO A PROCESS LIKE THE ELBPHIL-
HARMONIE IN HAMBURG. AFTER YEARS OF
HARSH CRITICISMS, THE PEOPLE OF HAMBURG
ARE NOW SO ENTHUSIASTIC ABOUT THEIR 'ELPHI'
THAT IT HAS ITS OWN DAILY COLUMN IN THE
'ABENDBLATT'.

'Instead of individual spectacular buildings, Zurich offers a string of pearls of many different interesting buildings and places.'

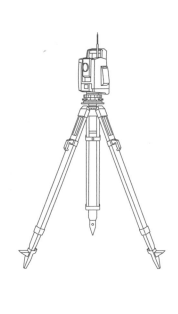

André Odermatt

It was a fierce referendum campaign and there were some major debates, but in the end the people of Zurich said yes. Perhaps part of the assimilation process already took place through these discussions. In any case they now get not one but two gifts: a very Zurich-like building by Chipperfield and a large new green space.

Christina Schumacher

Controversies are important and right when dealing with such major, expensive and complex buildings. Voicing criticisms and differing points of view is a tribute to what is an open-minded and democratic city. That's what also makes the process exciting.

André Odermatt

There are some people who argue that this produces mediocre results. I personally would definitely disagree. The Kunsthaus benefited enormously from the dialogue. You can see the same thing in the university district, which has likewise provoked vigorous controversy amongst the people living there and policymakers.

Christina Schumacher

What I find important is the discussion about the Bührle Collection. The city and cantonal governments commissioned a project to contextualise the collection, in order to show the historical origins of the collection and how it was financed. Again, this is about a discussion with the general public, about including them. To me that's typical for Zurich.

Anna Schindler

THE NEW KUNSTHAUS SUITS ZURICH, ON THAT WE AGREE, AND IT REPRESENTS ADDED WORTH FOR THE PEOPLE OF ZURICH. BUT WHEN IT COMES TO ASSIMILATING THE NEW URBAN SPACE, IT'S NOT JUST ABOUT THE POPULATION OF ZURICH. INSTEAD THE EXTENSION BUILDING IS MEANT TO ANCHOR ZURICH'S INTERNATIONAL STANDING AS A CITY OF CULTURE EVEN MORE FIRMLY.

André Odermatt

What we're talking about is location marketing as a city of culture and architecture. Zurich's architecture has a very good reputation. Perhaps it doesn't attract the broad mass of tourists, but it's definitely interesting for a specialist audience. A Kunsthaus alone doesn't necessarily boost this, but it's a further piece of the mosaic in what is a very attractive overall package. What I myself have noticed staying in other cities is that Zurich still has potential in the guided tour segment. At the moment things are very focused on the Old Town and on the cultural venues. But very few tourists go to the university district, for example, although the ETH and the university, with their publicly accessible interiors, have quite a lot to offer.

Christina Schumacher

There are a lot of interesting things open to the public in the university district that are almost unknown, for example the Zoological Museum or the Law Faculty Library by Santiago Calatrava. Instead of individual spectacular buildings, Zurich offers a string of pearls of many different interesting buildings and places.

André Odermatt

That's precisely one of the great qualities of our city, and equally so in its international positioning: it presents a tableau instead of stranded architectural UFOs.

'The building and its public character are stylistically indicative for the university district. They give an impression of what porosity can look like.'

43

Free Space for Zurich

AN ART MUSEUM
IS A SPACE
FOR POSSIBILITIES.

—
33 **Peter Haerle,**
Cultural Director, City of Zurich

The extension of the Kunsthaus Zürich in the heart of the city creates scope for ideas, for fantasies: What should happen here? What should be shown? And above all, which people and which topics will be given a voice in these rooms?

In the past everything was relatively simple: there was a director – exclusively in the form of a man – and there was perhaps a collections commission, who met behind closed doors to determine what would be shown in the Kunsthaus. There was a canon that dictated which art was important, which was then willingly accepted by the public. For decades the same pictures hung in the same places, thus avoiding any irritating surprises when a visitor strolled through the building again half a year later. The relationship between the museum and the public was top-down: up above, the sublime art; down below, an awed public.

Today's world is different, and museums have a new role to play. What that role is and how it should be achieved has to be constantly renegotiated and redefined. The institution has to be a cultural seismograph. This requires openness and a willingness to engage in dialogue – but without, in the process, being random.

In the context of globalisation society has become more diverse, and the classical canon has dissolved. People are asking questions, they have wishes and demands vis-à-vis an art museum: Where's the art by women? Where's the art from other cultural circles? Where's the digital art? Where's the local Zurich art? Or they are critically sceptical of the institution 'art museum' as a whole: What role does art play in society? What questions can it answer? What has art got to do with me?

The Kunsthaus extension is a huge chance to embrace these questions and to turn them into something artistically beneficial. To do so requires an inspired and zestful commitment from the managers and board of the institution to engage in a dialogue with all the stakeholders: curators, museum staff, artists and the public. The architectural framework to do so is ideal. Which location could be more suited to such an exchange than this spacious building with its expansive hall, forming Zurich's new piazza?

The museum is a free space that has been built BY the public FOR the public. Within and without its walls the power of conventions that determine, guide and sometimes constrain our everyday routines are suspended. The Kunsthaus – old and new – belongs to all of us, just as we are all part of it too.

CHRONOLOGY
2001 TO 2020

—

Compiled by Björn Quellenberg

20 01

—

THE EXPERT HEARING

In spring 2001 the Kunsthaus Zürich organises an international expert hearing to open up the reorientation process to the public at large, and launches a consultation lasting until 2010 to sound out opinion on the idea for an extension. The prevailing view among external contributors is that the Kunsthaus is ideally placed to embark on this transformation: its legal structure, the combination of a collection of national importance and exhibitions with international reach, strong popular support and the steadily growing membership of the Zürcher Kunstgesellschaft add up to a substantial case for the extension. The unanimity of the opinions expressed, which are shared by cultural policy-makers from the city and canton, confirms the Kunsthaus team's resolve to launch a project for an extension on Heimplatz.

THE OUTLINE PROPOSAL

In winter 2001 the directors and curators of the Kunsthaus draw up the outline proposal, which is unveiled to the public in May 2002 at a joint media briefing with the Stiftung Zürcher Kunsthaus and the incumbent mayor of Zurich. It sets out the rationale for the extension, prioritises a number of areas – collection and exhibitions, art education, the library and the restoration department – and proposes Heimplatz as the location.

20 02

—

THE URBAN PLANNING DEBATE

In summer 2002 the city's Building Surveyor's Office and the cantonal Building Authority stage a hearing on the future development of the university district, to which the Kunsthaus and the cantonal school site on Heimplatz belong. The Kunsthaus's wish to use the lower section of the school site is supported by a cantonal government decision of 6 March 2002, and by discussions between the mayor, the head of the city's Department of Justice and Home Affairs and the president of the Zürcher Kunstgesellschaft.

—

THE MCKINSEY STUDY

In autumn 2002 the directors compile a 'Preliminary Study of the Kunsthaus Extension', which is evaluated on a pro-bono basis by McKinsey & Company between August and October 2002, with extensive statistics being added. Essentially a feasibility study, it comprises three modules: business plan, funding (investment and follow-up costs) and the communications strategy.

20 03

—

THE KUNSTHAUS EXTENSION PROJECT

Work on optimising the initial blueprint begins in spring 2003, in collaboration with the new programme committee. The amendments concern the following factors: reassigning some floor areas to the collection/exhibitions, structuring, content aspects and concision of form.

20 05

—

LEGISLATIVE GOAL: EXTENSION

The Kunsthaus extension is adopted as a legislative goal of the city government. As part of a location strategy the canton decides to move the Zurich University of Teacher Education to the city centre area around the main station. The Kunsthaus can now push ahead with its plans for an extension on the site next to the cantonal school.

20 07

—

29 August 2007

A DECISIVE TURNING POINT

The canton guarantees the Kunsthaus the cantonal school site as a location for the future extension. The architectural competition receives an explicit go-ahead before the real estate deal is notarised. The last stone falls into place when the city government approves a project credit in its first session following the summer break. The transaction makes its way through the relevant political bodies, namely the city parliament and the advisory committee. With the first tranche of the credit paid out, the competition can get underway and the preliminary project can be elaborated.

At the first press conference for the Kunsthaus extension, held on 29 August 2007 in the lecture hall to coincide with the publication of the city government's decision, the steering committee sets out the project's main points and the next steps.

The Kunsthaus extension is to be tailored to the museum's artistic content, as well as by long-term considerations, which gives rise to its spatial design and in turn constitutes the core of the competition brief for participating architects.

—

14 December 2007

THE ARCHITECTURAL COMPETITION IS LAUNCHED

Advertisements in trade journals and online platforms invite architectural offices from around the world to apply to take part in the competition, to run from 14 December 2007 to 1 February 2008.

From the anticipated large number of applications, an international jury selects 20 suitable teams to take part in the anonymous competition. The jury is presided over by Walter B. Kielholz as chairman and is moderated by Prof. Carl Fingerhuth.

20 08

—

March 2008

RESPONSE TO THE ARCHITECTURAL COMPETITION AND GRANTING OF THE PROJECT PLANNING CREDIT

With 214 applications from architectural offices from 22 countries, the Kunsthaus extension project in Zurich awakens international interest. In early March a panel of 20 experts selects 20 teams to take part in the one-step competition. Nine of the participating offices come from Switzerland, eight from Europe and three from outside Europe. In early April the participants – who are working anonymously and include renowned and seasoned architects, as well as two young talent teams – are comprehensively briefed, largely on the basis of the competition programme.

The process chosen guarantees fair treatment of all the participants until the selection of a winning project in November 2008.

The City of Zurich is a supporter of the project, with the city parliament ratifying a project credit of 6.5 million francs, applied for by the city government in autumn 2007, by a vote of 113 to 3 on 26 March 2008.

—

30 October 2008

THE EXTENSION IS GIVEN A LABEL

The Zurich agency Büro4 is commissioned to give an overall design to the construction reports, residents' information sheets, documentation stands, site hoardings, posters, invitations, fundraising brochures and inauguration publications during the entire period of the project. A year later the design wins the agency the coveted Red Dot Design Award.

—

7 November 2008
DAVID CHIPPERFIELD ARCHITECTS WIN THE COMPETITION

The jury declares the project submitted by David Chipperfield Architects to be the winner of the competition to design the extension to the Kunsthaus Zürich.

15 December 2008
PRESENTATION OF THE WINNING PROJECT

David Chipperfield Architects' winning project is a striking formulation of the plan for a 21st-century museum to meet the demands of art and the general public alike. The Kunsthaus extension's partners present it at a media conference on 15 December 2008. The international jury find that the pristine elegance of the British architect's design offers the best solution to the content and urban-planning requirements stipulated in the competition programme. According to the jury's report, the extension building will serve both the art world and the public well.

From 16 December 2008 until 11 January 2009 all 20 competition entries are exhibited in the lecture hall of the Kunsthaus Zürich.

20 09
—

24 September 2009
MORE OPEN, GREENER, BETTER: THE RE-WORKING

David Chipperfield Architects' winning design is optimised in line with the jury's recommendations in terms of its role within the fabric of the city and with regard to its internal organisation. The revision addresses all of the recommendations made by the jury. The future principal clients are now presented with a project that is more open, greener and better: in a word, feasible.

—

27 October 2009
A PROJECT PARTNERSHIP IS FORMED FOR THE KUNSTHAUS EXTENSION

At the conclusion of the architectural competition, the organising committee restructures itself into a simple project partnership. Partners, and hence principals, are the City of Zurich, the Zürcher Kunstgesellschaft and the Stiftung Zürcher Kunsthaus.

With the establishment of the Einfache Gesellschaft Kunsthaus-Erweiterung (EGKE), the public and private partners in the Kunsthaus extension set up an organisation to coincide with the beginning of the project-planning phase. With the goal of realising the extension building on Heimplatz, the EGKE is responsible for developing the private design plans, securing the financing, overseeing the construction project and is in charge of public relations.

—

20 10
—

14 April 2010
THE ZURICH CITY GOVERNMENT APPROVES AN INCREASE OF THE PLANNING CREDIT

The Kunsthaus extension project clears a major hurdle: with 99 to 3 votes the city parliament agrees to the city government's request to increase the project credit from 6.5 to 18 million francs. This amount is earmarked for detailed cost estimates, the documentation for the building application and the elaboration of the concept plans.

—

18 October 2010
FORMING OF THE FÖRDERSTIFTUNG KUNSTHAUS-ERWEITERUNG

The Zürcher Kunstgesellschaft commits itself to contributing 75 million francs in private funds to the Kunsthaus extension, to which end it creates a foundation for the collection of donations. Its purpose: booking incoming funds, supervising their use in keeping with the statutes – exclusively to finance the extension – and ensuring the provision to donors of all tax advantages associated with donating to the foundation. President of the foundation board is lawyer Franz J. Kessler. The first phase involves accepting major donations from foundations and business enterprises.

This act represents the fundraising kick-off, the goals being tailored upwards proportionally to the costs. Due to the personal efforts of Thomas W. Bechtler, Walter B. Kielholz, Conrad P. Schwyzer, Conrad M. Ulrich, Gitti Hug, Anne Keller, Christoph Becker, as well as Renato Fassbind, Adrian Hagenbach, Elisabeth Oltramare, Herbert Scheidt, Nicola von Lutterotti-Scheidt and Susanne von Meiss, some 88 million francs are collected from private donors by the time the extension opens.

—

9 November 2010
THE DESIGN PLANS ARE MADE PUBLIC

The design plans for the extension building are presented, from 10 November until 24 January 2011, to allow public discussions to take place. Following this participatory process, eventual objections are collected, processed and incorporated into a report for the city parliament.

20 11
—

26 January 2011
45 OBJECTIONS TO THE DESIGN PLANS ARE SUBMITTED

Forty-five separate objections are submitted to the planned design, many of which contain the same demand: that the planned new building should be set back several metres.

Because so many of the submissions involve the same issue, the city decides to forge contacts with the 'Open Pfauen' group. The city authorities examine all of the submissions, and in the event that if they decide to reject a demand they are obliged to justify it in the form of a report, that is then presented to the city parliament together with the design plan.

—

6 September 2011
THE PRELIMINARY DESIGN PROJECT IS APPROVED, THE BUSINESS PLAN IS PRESENTED

The preliminary design project for the extension to the Kunsthaus Zürich is complete. The design by David Chipperfield's team of architects has assumed its definitive form. The timetable anticipates the project to be voted on by the electorate in 2012, with the opening of the Kunsthaus extension planned for 2017. The new building will create space for crowd-pulling temporary exhibitions and a dynamic presentation of the post-1960 art collection and the new emphasis on French painting and Impressionism.

During the preliminary design project, the basic architectural concept of the winning design is refined and adapted to meet the future uses. Further details are also added to the timetable and the cost estimate for the realisation of the project. The cost target stands at 178.8 million francs. In line with the recommendations made by the building committee, the overall dimensions of the above-ground and below-ground volumes are reduced in scale and the forecourt area facing Heimplatz is enlarged, making the size of the new building smaller than originally envisaged vis à-vis the cityscape.

The Kunsthaus, in its capacity as occupant and operator, presents the key points of its business plan. The forecasted additional costs are to be covered by maintaining the existing high level of self-funding at over 50% in combination with the increased subsidy set out in the City of Zurich's cultural mission statement.

—

12 December 2011
THE CANTONAL PARLIAMENT APPROVES 30 MILLION AND THE SITE OCCUPANCY

The Canton of Zurich supports the Kunsthaus Zürich extension project with 30 million francs. With 154 votes to one, the cantonal parliament approves the contribution from the Lottery Fund to the Stiftung Zürcher Kunsthaus. It also provides the necessary development site, valued at 15 million francs, as an 80-year leasehold.

—

14 December 2011
MUNICIPAL CONTRIBUTION AND LAYOUT PLAN

The city government files an application with the city parliament to be approved by the electorate for an investment contribution of

88 million francs and to take a 5-million-franc share of the non-recurring preliminary expenditures for the extension. The city government requests an increased annual municipal contribution of 7.5 million francs to cover the running and value upkeep of the extension building, starting in 2017. Simultaneously, the city government presents the public plans for the overall site of the Kunsthaus extension for the city parliament to consult and decide upon.

20 12

—

23 April 2012

KUNSTHAUS ZÜRICH JOINS FORCES WITH THE FONDATION HUBERT LOOSER

The Kunsthaus Zürich receives an outstanding private collection of modern and contemporary art in the form of the Hubert Looser Collection. Focusing on Abstract Expressionism, Minimal Art and Arte Povera, 70 works are to be housed in the Kunsthaus extension as a long-term loan, ideally complementing the museum's own holdings.

The Looser Collection evinces a stance that abjures modish trends, choosing instead to foster dialogues and positive dichotomies, and in so doing generates encounters replete with new experiences and revelations. This is perfectly in tune with the Kunsthaus's goal of dynamically presenting its own collection in the Heimplatz ensemble.

—

28 May 2012

THE EMIL BÜHRLE COLLECTION COMES TO THE KUNSTHAUS ZÜRICH

The Zürcher Kunstgesellschaft signs an agreement with the Foundation E.G. Bührle Collection, setting out the terms and conditions for the long-term loan of some 190 paintings and sculptures to the Kunsthaus Zürich. The internationally renowned collection of the industrialist Emil Bührle (1890–1956) is to be exhibited in the extension to the Kunsthaus Zürich. This move creates the largest assembly of French Impressionist paintings in Europe outside Paris. The new agreement between the Foundation E.G. Bührle Collection and the Zürcher Kunstgesellschaft replaces the agreement in principle drawn up in February 2006, thus setting the seal on the intent, declared by the parties at the time, to make the artworks from the Bührle Collection publically accessible in the new Kunsthaus extension. In addition to the participatory credit for construction investments and subsidies for the kick-off costs of the Kunsthaus extension, the related costs and income are included in the subsidy requests to be addressed by the Zurich city parliament in July 2012.

—

29 May 2012 / 12 June 2012

APPROVAL BY ADVISORY COMMITTEE

On 12 June 2012 the city parliament's advisory committee approves the municipal contribution to the Kunsthaus extension building. The corresponding thumbs-up from the Building Committee had already been given two weeks earlier.

—

4 July 2012

CITY PARLIAMENT VOTES YES

With a large majority, the Zurich city parliament approves the financing and the design plan for the Kunsthaus extension.

—

28 September 2012

FORMING OF THE BALLOT COMMITTEE

A few days after 25 November 2012 is fixed as the date for the general vote, an independent, non-partisan ballot committee is formed to promote the Kunsthaus extension. Over 160 political, civic, business and cultural figures give the seminal project their backing and make their support known on their own website.

—

5 October 2012

MAJOR EXHIBITION

Running until 6 January 2013, the Kunsthaus Zürich stages the exhibition 'The New Kunsthaus – Great Art and Architecture', covering over 1,300 square metres and showcasing the amenities and highlights that the extension would offer to the public.

—

25 November 2012

ZURICH'S ELECTORATE GIVE THEIR APPROVAL TO THE EXTENSION PROJECT

The result of the referendum of 25 November 2012 is a major success for Zurich as a city of culture and the Zürcher Kunstgesellschaft alike. With a vote of 53.9% for and 46.1% against, a majority of the population give their stamp of approval to the idea of a museum for art and audiences in the 21st century.

20 12

—

16 March 2013

DESIGN PLAN COMES INTO FORCE

On 31 January 2013 the Canton of Zurich Building Department approves the public design plans for the Kunsthaus extension, set to come into force on 16 March 2013.

—

25 March 2013

MAJOR DONATION TOWARDS THE EXTENSION

The Walter Haefner Foundation underwrites its support for the extension to the Kunsthaus Zürich with a donation of 20 million francs.

—

16 April 2013

INSTALLATION OF A FACADE MODEL

A full-scale model of the facade of the Kunsthaus extension is erected on the site, allowing different variations of the materialisation of the prospective facade to be tried and tested. The installation is temporary and the samples shown are not per se identical to the final outcome.

—

31 May 2013

BUILDING PERMISSION GRANTED

At its meeting on 31 May 2013 the Building Division of the Zurich city government approves the building permit for the Kunsthaus extension. The permit is subject to the customary conditions for projects of this magnitude. Appeals have to be lodged within 30 days.

20 15

—

2 February 2015

BUILDING PERMISSION TAKES LEGAL EFFECT

Legal disputes block progress on the development of the extension to the Zürcher Kunsthaus for two years. The Lucerne-based Archicultura Foundation lodges a legal challenge against the 31 May 2013 decision to grant building permission. On 19 December 2014 the Building Appeals Court rejects the appeal, making the building permit final.

—

3 August 2015

CONSTRUCTION COMMENCES

The preliminary preparatory work on the construction site begins on 3 August 2015, marking the start of the implementation phase of the project by David Chipperfield's architectural team. If construction proceeds according to schedule the extension is set to open in 2020.

The existing gymnastics halls and the huts on the site are freed of contaminated substances prior to demolition. At the same time the trees to be retained for the art garden are safeguarded, while the remainder are cleared. Hoardings are erected, after which excavation work begins.

20 16

—

May 2016

CONSTRUCTION WORK ON THE PASSAGE

Building work on the underground passageway running under Heimplatz starts. After the opening the passage will enable visitors to circulate between the Chipperfield building and the existing ensemble – unimpeded by the volume of traffic on Heimplatz or the weather. The passageway also serves as a route for artworks to be moved, transported from the depots into the collection and exhibition rooms from opposite sides of the street.

Apart from a few weekend closures, Heimplatz remains open to traffic, which is re-routed according to the individual phases of the construction work.

—

24 August 2016

EXCAVATION WORKS ARE COMPLETED

As anticipated, the earthworks have revealed the entrenchment wall of the town's fortifications dating from the 17th century. No remains from the ancient Jewish cemetery are found. The earthworks for the Kunsthaus extension are closely monitored by city archaeologists.

—

8 November 2016

LAYING OF THE FOUNDATION STONE

The commissioning body – represented by Walter B. Kielholz (President of the Zürcher Kunstgesellschaft), Corine Mauch (Mayor of Zurich, Vice President of the EGKE), Dr. Christoph Becker (Director of the Kunsthaus Zürich), Dr. Martin Zollinger (President of the Stiftung Zürcher Kunsthaus) and Dr. André Odermatt (City Councillor, Head of the Department of Planning and Building) – lay the foundation stone of the Kunsthaus Zürich extension together with architect Sir David Chipperfield. Urs Fischer, the internationally renowned Zurich artist, provides an artistic cornerstone for the collection in the expanded Kunsthaus in the form of a bronze sculpture measuring over 2 x 2 metres.

20
17

—

14 March 2017

PARTIAL CLOSING FOR BUILDING WORK

The construction work on the Kunsthaus extension reaches the existing buildings. The museum stays open and operational: new stairs and lifts are installed; the new access routes lead from the existing entrance hall down to the passageway to the extension building on the other side of Heimplatz; the auditorium opposite the restaurant serves as a temporary entrance hall. Works by Alberto Giacometti are moved from the ground floor to the upper storeys. Art education services are not affected by the reconstruction work.

20
18

—

26 April 2018

PASSAGEWAY BREAKTHROUGH

The last layer of earth between the 82-metre-long passage from the extension and the existing building by Karl Moser is breached.

3 July 2018

A MILESTONE: COMPLETION OF THE STRUCTURAL SHELL

The vision of a museum for the 21st century – the new Kunsthaus – assumes a concrete form: the completion of the shell means that the full dimensions and proportions of the building can be appreciated for the first time. For many years the extension building had existed only in the form of plans and models; now the building has reached its full height and as a whole now shapes the face of Heimplatz. The completion of the shell comes almost three years after construction began. The building work is advancing on schedule.

—

24 May 2018

NEW LONG-TERM LOAN: THE MERZBACHER COLLECTION

The collection of Gabriele and Werner Merzbacher is to move into the Kunsthaus extension on long-term loan. Under the terms of an agreement between the Kunstgesellschaft and the collectors a total of 65 works are promised to the Kunsthaus for at least 20 years, comprising paintings by the great masters of Impressionism, Post-Impressionism and Fauvism, and including members of the Brücke and Blauer Reiter groups. Following the Emil Bührle Collection and the Hubert Looser Collection, this is the third private collection to complement the Kunsthaus's own prestigious holdings.

20
19

—

17 July 2019

PUBLICATION OF OPENING SCENARIO

The completion of the extension is announced for winter 2020, with the opening of the museum scheduled in phases during 2021.

—

27 August 2019

THE MAIN ENTRANCE REOPENS

After two-and-a-half years of reconstruction, the main entrance to the Kunsthaus opens its doors again. The existing building is underpinned by a second basement level to accommodate the underground connection between the Moser and Chipperfield buildings.

20
20

—

29 February 2020

OPEN BUILDING SITE

On the fourth open-house day, which since 2017 has included allowing visitors to visit the building site, over 1,800 people tour the building, where the interior work is underway. The demand, including for the private building site tours on offer since September 2019, is larger than the limited capacity.

—

11 December 2020

KEY HANDOVER

After five years of building work, the Kunsthaus extension is completed. Some 230 personalities from politics, business and culture who were directly or indirectly involved in the project are invited to the key-handover ceremony. Representing the owners of the new property, Richard Hunziker, President of the Stiftung Zürcher Kunsthaus, accepts the key from the commissioning body. The President of the EGKE, Walter B. Kielholz, City Mayor Corine Mauch, Dr. André Odermatt, Head of the Department of Planning and Building and the architect Sir David Chipperfield address the gathered guests and present the overall balance of the project, which has been completed for less than the set cost ceiling of 206 million francs.

—

12/13 December 2020

THREE-PHASE OPENING

With its inauguration, the building designed by David Chipperfield Architects presents itself as an architectural masterwork. On two visiting days the general public is invited to experience the new spaces, their proportions and sedate materialisation. In the evening the second part of Pipilotti Rist's installation 'Tactile Lights' is inaugurated. The projection wanders across the facades of the Kunsthaus and the Schauspielhaus, creating a 360-degree-panorama artistic event. A little time is still required for the Kunsthaus to have everything fully up and running. Following a test phase, the art will move into the extension in summer 2021, before complete operations finally commence on 9 October 2021.

—

A House for
the Public

Zürcher Kunstgesellschaft
(88 mil.)

Canton of Zurich
(30 mil.)

City of Zurich
(88 mil.)

WHAT DOES THE NEW KUNSTHAUS COST – AND WHO IS PAYING FOR WHAT?

The Kunsthaus Zürich is sustained by the Stiftung Zürcher Kunsthaus and the Zürcher Kunstgesellschaft. The Zürcher Kunstgesellschaft is responsible for the running of the Kunsthaus. With over 20,000 members it is one of the largest art associations in Europe. The Stiftung Zürcher Kunsthaus owns the properties and is responsible for the upkeep of the buildings. The City of Zurich, for its part, makes annual contributions to both institutions, which have been increased with the extension.

In order to realise the extension building, the three parties formed the Einfache Gesellschaft Kunsthaus-Erweiterung, which has assumed the role of the commissioning body. Once the construction work has been completed, the extension will be transferred to the Stiftung Zürcher Kunsthaus.

The budget for the extension totals 206 million francs, of which – thanks to the commitment of many private art lovers – the Zürcher Kunstgesellschaft has been able to contribute 88 million francs. The City of Zurich has contributed an identical sum, while the Canton of Zurich has injected 30 million francs from the Lottery Fund and has additionally made the building land available in the form of a free leasehold.

The broadly based financing is testimony to the fact that the Zürcher Kunsthaus is a house for the public.